Puffins

Victoria Blakemore

vblakemore.author@gmail.com

Copyright info/picture credits

Cover, LouieLea/Shutterstock; Page 3, jon57/Pixabay; Page 5, Pexels/Pixabay; Page 7, max5128/AdobeStock; Page 9, susanne906/Pixabay; Pages 10-11, hstiver/AdobeStock; Page 13, DesignFife/Pixabay; Page 15, Decokon/Pixabay; Page 17, jon57/Pixabay; Page 19, jon57/Pixabay; Page 21, Frank Fichtmüller/AdobeStock; Page 23; DesignFife/Pixabay; Page 25, StockSnap/Pixabay; Page 27, jon57/Pixabay; Page 29, DesignFife/Pixabay; Page 31, de_zigeuner/Pixabay; Page 33, LouieLea/Shutterstock

Table of Contents

What Are Puffins?

Puffins are small birds. They look very similar to penguins, but they are not related to them. They are members of the Auk family, like murres and guillemots.

There are four kinds of puffins. They differ in size, color, and where they live.

The Atlantic puffin is the most common puffin. Other puffins include the horned puffin, tufted puffin, and the rhinoceros auklet.

Size

Puffin range in size. The Atlantic puffin is the smallest puffin. It grows to be about ten inches tall. The tufted puffin is the largest. It can grow to be about sixteen inches tall.

When fully grown, puffins often weigh between one and two pounds.

Male puffins are usually larger

than female puffins.

Physical Characteristics

Puffin beaks are very brightly colored in the spring and summer. The colors fade in the winter.

Puffin feathers are **waterproof**. This helps them to stay dry and warm when they are swimming or diving in the ocean.

The tufted puffin has long

yellow **tufts** of feathers along

the sides of their head.

Habitat

Puffins are found along rocky coasts and on islands. They also spend a lot of their time in the ocean.

They prefer rocky coasts because the spaces between the rocks make good places for them to build burrows.

Range

Puffins are found along the coasts of North America, Europe, and Asia.

Many are seen in countries such as Canada, the United States, Greenland, and Norway.

Diet

Puffins are **carnivores**. They eat

only meat.

Their diet is made up of fish and

crustaceans. They usually catch

fish such as herring, capelin,

sand lance, and cod. They also

eat some kinds of shrimp,

mollusks, and marine worms.

Puffin beaks can open very wide.

This allows them to carry about

many small fish at a time.

Puffins have small **spines** inside their beak. These help to hold the fish they catch in place. Diving to find food can take a lot of energy. Puffins need to be able to catch many fish each time.

They can dive as deep as two hundred feet below the surface to catch fish.

Puffins spend most of the winter

out at sea. They dive and swim

to catch their food.

Communication

Puffins use mainly sound and movement to communicate with each other. Chicks use a peeping sound to ask for food. Puffins also make a deep growling call.

The **position** of the head, wings, and feet can send a message to other puffins.

When puffins land, they spread their wings, stand on one foot, and lower their head. This tells other puffins that they are not a threat.

17

Movement

Puffins have a special way they swim underwater. They use their wings to **propel** them and their feet to steer. It looks like they are flying. They can dive and stay under for about one minute.

Puffins can fly at speeds of up to about fifty-five miles per hour.

They are able to flap their wings about four hundred times per minute, which helps them to fly so fast.

Puffin Chicks

Puffins lay one egg each year.

The mother and father take turns

sitting on the egg until it hatches.

It can take about six weeks to

hatch.

Puffin chicks are called pufflings.

They are born with soft, fluffy

feathers. Their feathers become

more smooth as they get older.

Puffin parents work together to bring food back to their puffling. The puffling is ready to leave the burrow after about eight weeks.

Puffin Life

Puffins are very social birds. They spend most of their time in large groups. A group of puffins is called a colony or a puffinry.

Colonies **gather** on coasts and islands in the spring and summer. They meet to lay eggs and raise chicks.

Puffins often come back to the same burrow to lay their egg each year.

Puffin Burrows

Puffins dig burrows with their feet and bills. They usually pick areas that are along cliffs or between rocks. They line the back of the burrow with feathers for their nest.

Puffins are very **protective** of their burrows. They are often seen standing guard outside.

24

Puffins tuck their beak into their chest when they pass another burrow. This is a sign that they are just passing and mean no harm.

25

Population

Puffins are not **endangered**, but their populations are **declining**. The Atlantic puffin is listed as **vulnerable**. It could soon be **endangered**.

The other three kinds of puffins could also become **endangered** if their populations continue to **decline**.

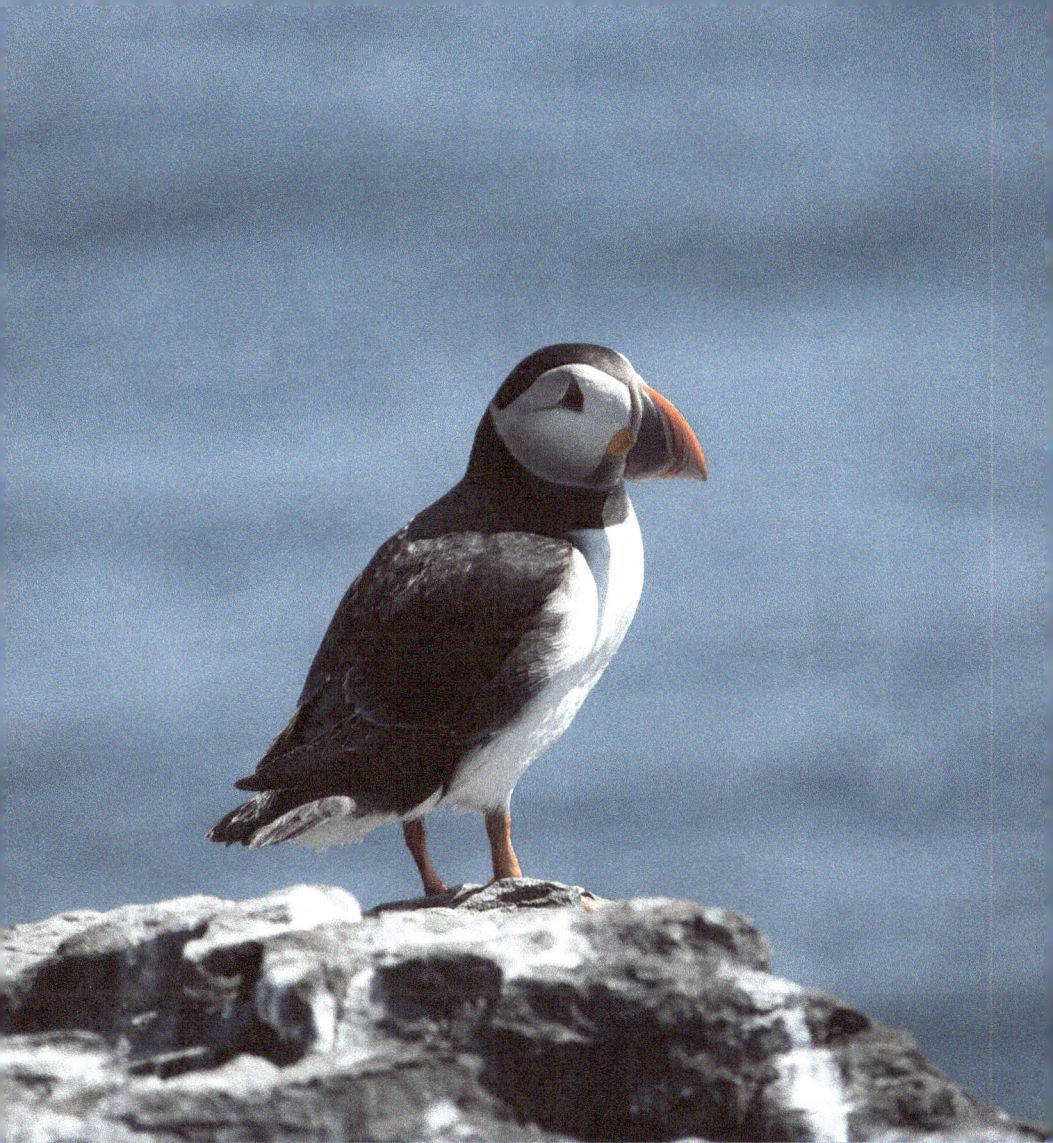

Puffins often live to be between

five and ten years old in the

wild. The oldest known puffin

lived to be thirty-six. **27**

Puffins in Danger

Puffins are facing many threats in the wild. Most of these threats come from humans. The main threat is habitat loss.

Puffin habitats are being destroyed by **pollution**, changes in temperature, and oil spills. **Overfishing** has made it hard for many puffins to find food.

Puffins have been hunted for their meat, feathers, and eggs. They are also **vulnerable** to disease and predators.

Helping Puffins

Puffins have been brought back to areas where they were once hunted. This was done by raising chicks there. The chicks returned to lay eggs when they were older.

Special protected areas provide animals such as puffins with safe habitats.

In some places, laws protect

puffins from being hunted.

There are also laws that try to

stop **overfishing**.

Some groups focus on research

and education. They want to

learn more about puffins so

they can find new ways to help

them.

Glossary

Carnivore: an animal that eats only meat

Crustaceans: an animal with a hard, jointed shell such as a crab, lobster, or shrimp

Declining: getting smaller

Endangered: at risk of becoming extinct

Gather: to collect or bring together

Overfishing: when too many of a kind of fish are caught and the population declines

Pollution: poisons, wastes, or other materials that can harm the environment

Position: the way something is placed

Propel: to push forward

Protective: likely to protect

Spines: sharp, pointed parts

Tuft: a group of long strands

Vulnerable: open to threat or harm, when an animal may become endangered

Waterproof: not letting water through

About the Author

Victoria Blakemore is a first grade

teacher in Southwest Florida with a

passion for reading.

You can visit her at

www.elementaryexplorers.com

Also in This Series

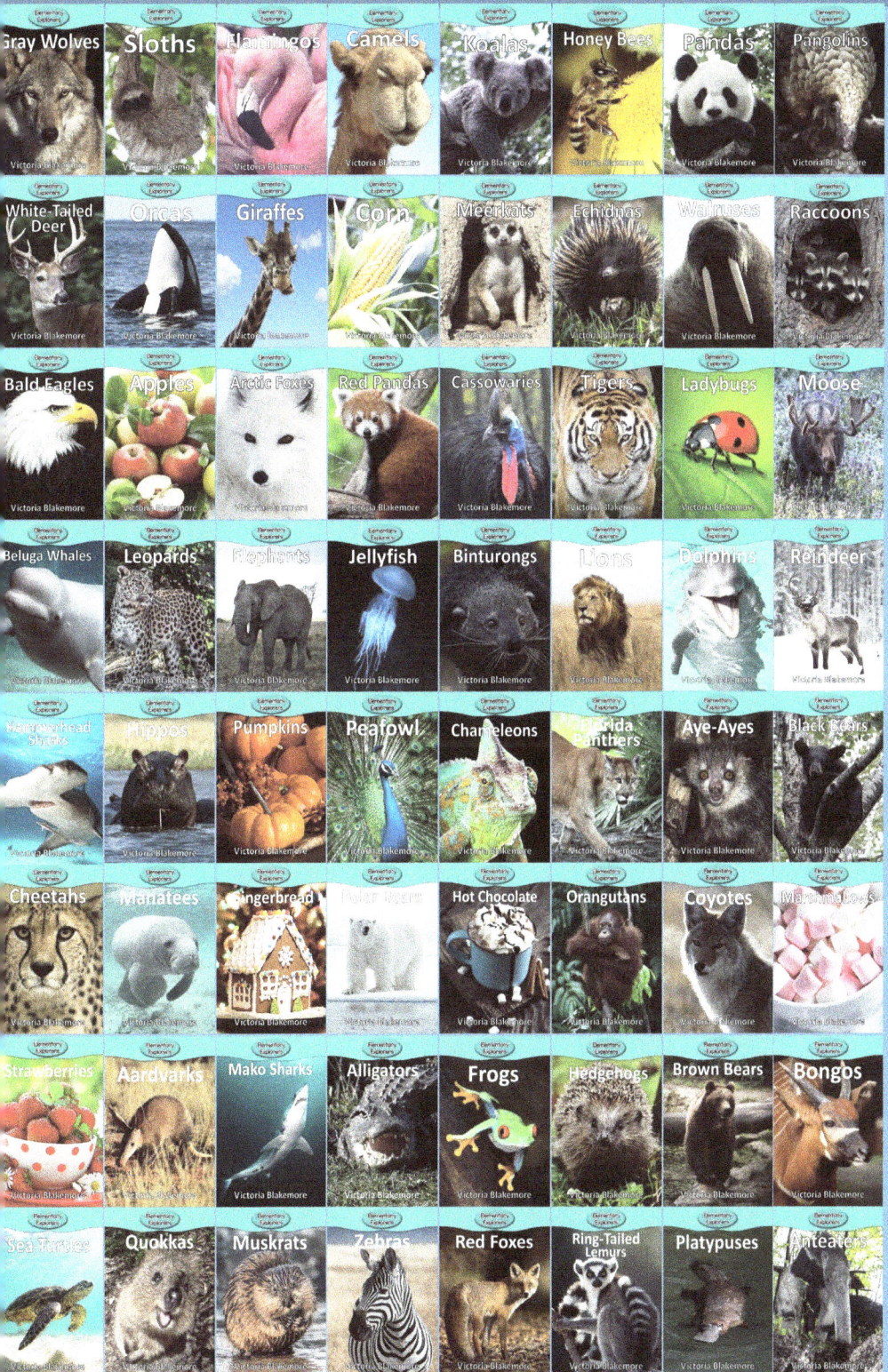

Gray Wolves	Sloths	Flamingos	Camels	Koalas	Honey Bees	Pandas	Pangolins
White-Tailed Deer	Orcas	Giraffes	Corn	Meerkats	Echidnas	Walruses	Raccoons
Bald Eagles	Apples	Arctic Foxes	Red Pandas	Cassowaries	Tigers	Ladybugs	Moose
Beluga Whales	Leopards	Elephants	Jellyfish	Binturongs	Lions	Dolphins	Reindeer
Hammerhead Sharks	Hippos	Pumpkins	Peafowl	Chameleons	Florida Panthers	Aye-Ayes	Black Bears
Cheetahs	Manatees	Gingerbread	Polar Bears	Hot Chocolate	Orangutans	Coyotes	Marshmallows
Strawberries	Aardvarks	Mako Sharks	Alligators	Frogs	Hedgehogs	Brown Bears	Bongos
Sea Turtles	Quokkas	Muskrats	Zebras	Red Foxes	Ring-Tailed Lemurs	Platypuses	Anteaters

Also in This Series

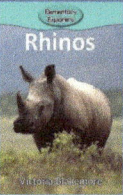

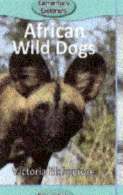

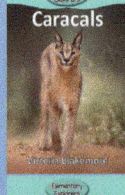

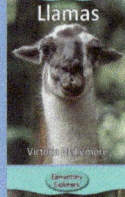

Kangaroos	Rhinos	Jaguars	Wombats	Capybaras	Gorillas	Cats	Skunks
Butterflies	Dingoes	Snow Leopards	African Wild Dogs	Penguins	Whale Sharks	Wolverines	Warthogs
Caracals	Badgers	Seals	Hummingbirds	Pikas	Humpback Whales	Pumas	Lemonade
Llamas	Tulips	Ostriches	Sunflowers	Fennec Foxes	Sea Lions	Squirrels	Roses
Porcupines	Ice Cream	Cotton Candy	Chocolate	Hyenas	Toucans	Saigas	Puffins

www.ingramcontent.com/pod-product-compliance
Lightning Source LLC
Chambersburg PA
CBHW051253020426

42333CB00025B/3188